Contents

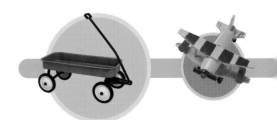

Sorting toys

✦ Collect some toys that move.

✦ How many different ways can you sort the toys?

YOU NEED:

toys that move

fast

slow

pull

push

✦ What other ways can you think of?

Changing playdough

YOU NEED:

playdough

✤ Use your playdough to make different things.

✤ Write down the actions you used to make them. Use Task Sheet 1.

I made...	Actions I used
sausages	push squeeze pull stretch twist

Task 3 P.E. forces

When you do P.E. at school you use forces.

✴ Think about which forces you use when you do these things.

kick a ball

throw a bean bag

hit a ball

climb a rope

jump on a trampoline

✴ Complete Task Sheet 2.

Tell the story

⭐ What actions do you use when you go down a slide?

⭐ Tell the story of going down a slide.

⭐ What do you have to do to start off, go faster, slow down, and stop?

Start off

Go faster

Slow down

Stop

5

Task 5 Best surface

Children in Class 2 want to know which surface is best for racing cars.

YOU NEED:

different surfaces

Here are their ideas.

How will we know which is the best?

We could push cars over different surfaces.

We could measure how far they went.

We need to push them the same way.

6

✴ Use your own ideas and the ideas from the children to find out:

Which surface is best for racing cars?

✴ Use Task Sheet 3 to help you plan a fair test.

✴ Record your results on Task Sheet 4.

Task 6 Down the ramp

Class 2 sent cars down a ramp.
They changed the height of the ramp to see if it made a difference to how far the car went.

Here is what they found out.

Height of ramp	How far the car goes
2 bricks	45 cm
3 bricks	70 cm
4 bricks	85 cm
5 bricks	100 cm
6 bricks	150 cm
7 bricks	180 cm

The table tells us that the higher the ramp the further the car goes along the floor.

How do you think Class 2 did their test?

Put your ideas on Task Sheet 5.

Make a plan and try it out.

Were your results like Class 2's?

Story of a graph

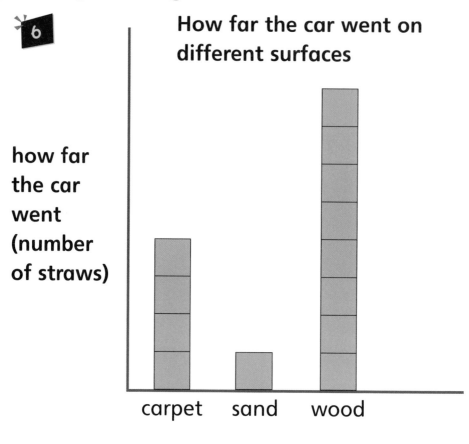

How far the car went on different surfaces

how far the car went (number of straws)

carpet   sand   wood

type of surface

⚡ Look at this graph.

⚡ Answer the questions on Task Sheet 6.

The questions help you to tell the story of the graph.

Stopping cars

✿ Use the story of the graph in Task 7 to help you plan a fair test to answer this question.

> *Which is the best surface to put at the bottom of a ramp for stopping cars?*

✿ Carry out your plan.

✿ What did you find out?

Super scooters

✵ What forces do you have to use when you are riding a scooter?

✵ Tell the story of Ben on his scooter. Write what he has to do when he needs to:

stop	slow down
change direction	go faster

Bikes and blades

✿ Tell the story of you playing on your bike or roller blades.

✿ Show what you do when you have to:

change direction	slow down
go faster	stop

⭐ Make a book about using forces in action.

⭐ Draw pictures or take digital photographs.

⭐ Name the forces and write what
happened in each picture.

Spot the forces

✦ How many forces in action can you see in this picture?

✦ Circle them on Task Sheet 7.

15

Race Track

We had lots of fun
When we made a bike track,
That went from the shed
To our house and back.
We pushed on the pedals
To make our bikes go,
Pushing hard to move fast;
Soft to go slow.
We turned left and right
At a tyre roundabout,
Then pulled on the brakes
When our breath ran out.

How do the riders speed
up, slow down and stop?